Linda Mason's

Doubtful Denise
Book #4

A Spirit of Truth Storybook

Copyright Page
Doubtful Denise
Book #4
A Spirit of Truth Storybook
Author: Linda C. Mason
Published by: Linda C. Mason
P. O. Box 1162
Powhatan, VA 23139
LMasonOnTop@aol.com
www.BooksByLMason.com

ISBN-13: 978-1-62217-367-9
ISBN-10: 1622173678

Registration # **TXu 1-925-200**
Illustrated by Jessica Mulles
Edited by Tamara Mason

Printed in the United States of America.

Doubtful Denise

One hot summer day, after eating a big breakfast of hot strawberry pancakes with blueberries and walnut syrup, bacon, eggs, and hash browns, I got up from the table and headed to my room to pack for summer camp. My dad was taking me to meet my friends. All of my friends were going this summer; Sarah, Bryan, EJ, Alison, Ping, and Gloria, my best friend. I couldn't wait to get all packed, but I doubted if I would remember everything I needed to take. Whenever I went anywhere, even to school, I would always forget something. Daddy had asked me to start writing myself a list so that I would stop forgetting things all the time, but I never remembered to make a list.

It has just been my daddy and me living in the big house for the last five years. My dad and I have gotten along pretty well with my grandma's help. Since Mommy and Daddy's divorce, I haven't seen or heard much from Mommy. She married another man and moved far away. I get a card on my birthday and a package for Christmas, but that was kind of it. I wonder if she thinks about us while she is busy with her new family. I miss her sometimes, but Daddy and I are super close, and he is a great parent. That's just the way it is, so I accept it. Daddy and I have our friends and neighbors, and they are like a family for us, so things are okay. I doubt that I will get to see her again, but that's okay, too. For now, I had to get ready for camp.

I started upstairs to pack my suitcase, but I couldn't remember where it was.

"Daddy!" I yelled.

"I can't find my suitcase!"

"It's in your closet, sweetie," Daddy replied.

"I bet I won't find it, and if I *can* find it, I probably won't be able to reach it." I said doubtfully.

Second-guessing myself seemed to be a way of life for me lately. I was never sure about anything I did. I doubt I will get my packing list right, either. I looked in my closet, and there it was, way up high on the top shelf, out of my reach.

"Daddy, I *told* you I wouldn't be able to reach it! It's too high!" I said, rolling my eyes because I already knew this would happen.

My dad came into the room and looked in the closet. He saw the suitcase and pointed to the stepladder leaning against the wall.

"Honey, use your step ladder to reach it. You are getting older now and need to start doing more things for yourself, okay? I bet if you tried, you might surprise yourself with all you can do," Dad said with a grin.

"Can you do me a favor?" he asked.

"Sure, but I doubt I will be able to do it right," I said halfheartedly, as I lowered my eyes and fiddled with the bow on my shirt.

"Denise Marie? Look at me, please." Dad only called me Denise Marie when he was serious.

"When you have a task to complete, and you start doubting yourself and your ability to accomplish it, promise me you will ask yourself this instead -- *'What kind of help will I need to be able to accomplish this on my own?'* Can you remember to do that for me?" Dad asked, looking into my eyes so tenderly.

"I love you, sweetie. However, I need you to develop more confidence in your abilities. You are so smart."

"Okay, Daddy. I'll try," I said as I gave him a big hug.

"Now, did you write that list of things you need to take with you on the camping trip? If not, do that before you do anything else, okay?"

"Well … alright, I guess," I said, still doubting myself a bit.

"*Okay*?" Dad repeated.

"You can do it, and here is a piece of paper and pen for you to get started. When you are finished, do you mind showing that list to me?"

"I think …" I started to say and changed it in mid-sentence.

"Sure. You can see my list." I said, instead.

"I'll do it right now," I heard myself say with more confidence than I remember having before.

I sat on my bed and began thinking of everything I didn't want to forget to take with me.

"Okay – mmm -- I will need underwear, pajamas, toiletries, bathing suit, a towel ... I think that's all," I thought to myself.

"Oh yeah! My MP3 player, alarm clock, sleeping bag and pillow, my bug spray!" I said to myself, feeling accomplished, but I thought some more.

"Oh, my goodness! I forgot to include clothes! My jeans, shorts, tops and a sweater in case I get cold, some socks, tennis shoes, flip flops, board games, a digital camera, my little phonebook with emergency numbers. Oh, and also some snacks."

Wow! I had finally written a list for myself, and I even felt confident that I could pack my own suitcase without leaving anything this time. This confidence felt strange but really good. I held my head up a little higher and went running down the hall to get Dad.

"Daddy! Daddy!" I called out proudly. I just knew that my dad would be so proud of me and love my list.

When Dad saw my list, he lifted me off the floor, twirled me around in his arms, and gave me a big kiss on my cheek.

"That is absolutely an awesome list, baby girl! I'm so proud of you! Now, let's get those suitcases packed, and I'll meet you in the kitchen with a cooler for your snacks," Dad said with the biggest smile on his face.

"Do you remember the question I told you to ask yourself the next time you doubted your ability to accomplish something?"

"Yes, I do," I said with a newly found confidence.

"I will ask myself *what kind of help will I need to accomplish this task on my own?*"

"Now, sometimes, you will need other people's help. Don't be afraid to ask if you really do but first see how much you can do on your own, okay?" Daddy explained.

"Thank you, Daddy. You are the best dad E**VE**R!"

I ran off to my room a**n**d packed everything on my list except the snacks I would do downstairs. I checked off each item as I put them in the suitcase. My suitcase was packed so tight, and it was a little heavy too. It was a good thing my sleeping **b**ag and pillow didn't have to go into a suitcase because they sur**e**ly wouldn't fit.

As Dad and I finished packing all of the snacks, we carried everything to the car and drove to Mrs. Peedlebum's house, where all of my friends were meeting. She had a small bus and was going to drive us to camp.

Everyone loaded their things onto the bus and picked their seat partners.

"Gloria!   Gloria!" I exclaimed as I ran toward my best friend.

"Let's be seat partners, okay?"

"Duh, Denise. Who else would I be seat partners with?" She said with a huge smile on her face. All of our friends were there, but there were also a few kids we didn't know. After loading the bags, snacks, drinks, and camping gear onto the bus, we boarded the bus and sang crazy songs all the way to the campsite.

We unloaded and were assigned cabins. Gloria, Ping, and I were assigned to a cabin with two other girls we didn't know.

"Hey," I whispered to Ping.

"Do you know those girls?" "No," she replied. "But they seem nice, I guess."

"Yeah, well, I doubt they will want to be friends with us ... well, maybe just not me."

"Why would you say that, Denise?" Gloria asked as she overheard Ping and me whispering.

"You are a cool person, and I like you, so why wouldn't those girls like you, too?"

"Yeah," Ping chimed in.

"You were the first person in the whole school to speak to me when I transferred from Japan last year. I thought you were really nice."

I started to think about what my friends were telling me and then about my dad. He wouldn't want me to doubt myself. I decided then that I was going to be the first person to say hello to the new girls. I walked right over to them, stuck out my hand, and said,

"Hi. I'm Denise. It's nice to meet you both. We are going to have a blast this week! Are you ready?" The girls looked at each other, a bit puzzled about what to do. They looked over at Gloria and Ping, who were also a bit shocked by my confidence. Gloria and Ping began to smile as they saw I had put my doubts aside. Then one of the girls said,

"I'm Robinette. Glad to meet you, Denise. Yeah! It's time to make new friends!"

The week went by so fast, as we spent our days playing games, swimming, fishing, and making new friends. It felt so good to play and not worry about things and doubt myself. Anytime I started to doubt, I remembered my dad and his big smile and how good it felt when I took the chance to do things on my own. I tied my own fishing line and baited my own hook.

I swam for the first time without hanging onto the wall, and I even volunteered to say grace one night and wasn't even scared that I would forget what to say. When I needed help, I asked for it, and it turned out to be easier than I thought. This was such a memorable trip because I remembered to rethink every time I wanted to doubt myself. Even my friends noticed how much happier and open I was, now that I wasn't so doubtful. I really felt as though I had finally started to grow up a bit.

Our camp week flew b**y,** and the next thing I knew, we were headed back home. When we got back to Mrs. Peedlebum's house, we all unloaded our items, and my dad was there waiting to take me home. When I saw him, **o**ur eyes locked, and I smiled so big. I knew he would be very proud of how well things went at camp. Somehow, I knew that this week at camp was a new beginning for me.

"I love yo**u**, Dad," I said as we walked hand in hand to the car.

During dinner that night, we had my favorite dish --
Pineapple and Chicken Double Cheese Pizza. I told Dad all about
my newly found confidence and all the things I had experienced
at camp. I could tell that he was very proud of me.

As we were chatting, the telephone rang. Dad answered it
and after a few seconds, looked at me kind of strangely with a
tear in his eye. Then he handed the phone to me without saying
a word. I was puzzled by his expression at first, but as soon as I
said hello, I totally understood.

It was my mom on the phone. I think my heart skipped a beat and dropped right out of my chest. So many emotions began to flood my head, but I tried to remain calm and confident. I couldn't lose all I had learned during my camping trip.

I have always known that we were a bi-racial family. Maybe looking more like my mom and all of the comments from others that came with a situation like this, had been more than my mom could handle when I was firstborn. I don't know why she left us. For right now, I'd better concentrate.

"Hey, Honey. It's Mommy. I know it has been a long time since we have spoken and I'm so sorry about that. But something told me to give you a call today, and I am so glad I did. I've missed you."

I was speechless as tears ran down my face. I really didn't even recognize her voice, but I knew in my heart it was my mom.

"Your dad tells me that you still have two more weeks of summer vacation left. Would you like to go to Disney World for a week with me?" She asked.

I tried to speak, but nothing would come out.

"Hello? Denise?" I heard her ask. I finally said,

"Ar—ar—are you serious?! Really?! With you?!"

I couldn't believe what I was hearing, and how could this even be possible?! My mom broke the awkward moment and said,

"Honey, I know this is an unexpected request and even an unexpected phone call. Know that I love you and always have loved you so much, and I want us to talk soon, maybe even on our trip, if you are willing to join me. You must have hundreds of questions to ask me. It will be just you and me," Mom started sounding very sincere.

"Can I talk to my dad first?" I replied, still feeling very bizarre.

"Of course you can," Mom answered.

"Call me back to let me know what you decide, okay, sweetheart?"

Dad called her back later on that evening to tell her I could go. However, I really didn't feel like I knew her anymore. We all decided that Dad would go with us, but he would keep to himself so that Mom and I could have a chance to talk and bond, pretty much alone. He wanted to be near if I felt I needed him. It seemed so unreal, yet it was happening. I didn't know what the future held for my mom and me, but I was sure of one thing; instead of being doubtful, I felt a strange assurance that things would be getting better from now on. Confidence sure does go a long way.

The End

The Message of Encouragement Worksheet

(You may copy this page)

(Fill in the missing letters on a <u>separate sheet of paper</u> or here, if you own the storybook, to unlock your secret message)

Doubtful Denise

N _ _ _ _   _ _ _ g _ _   _ _ _ _   _ o _ _

_ _ e _ _   _ _ _ _   _ r _ a _ _   _ l _ _ _ .

i _   _ _ _   _ _ n   _ _ _ _ m   _ _ ,

_ v _ _   _ _ _ t _ _   t _ _ _ _ _   _ _ l _

_ _ _   a c _ _ _ _ _ .

www.BooksByLMason.com to find out other games, puzzles, finger puppets, and treasure hunts, located within each paperback storybook, in addition to five new youth suspense novels coming soon: *Beyond Your Control, 'Disappointment Meets Grace, Within My Reach, Are You Sure About This?, and All Grown Up but Still Learning.*

Spirit of Truth Storybook
Activity Page

1.   *After reading the story, ask yourself the following questions:*

- What did you like about the story?
- What would you change about the story?
- What could you have done to make things turn out differently?
- Can you think of a way to help others after reading this story?

2.   *Go back through the story pages and **decode** your **secret message**.*

- Write the message on the lines below.
- Send it to me through email: LMasonOnTop@gmail.com

I will send you back a personal comment. Be sure to include your gender and age.

A unique inspirational message has been coded throughout each story to help create *added focus*, and a visual tool for interactive participation and concentration.

Decode your secret message and send it to me, along with your name and age, through my personal email address at [LMasonOnTop@aol.com,](mailto:LMasonOnTop@aol.com) and you will receive a personal email response from me. Additionally, a bonus finger puppet activity, along with other goodies, awaits each reader in the back of every first edition storybook. An Editor's Edition of this 26 Storybook Collection is forthcoming, which will include all 26 stories in two volumes at which time, the Master's List of every inspirational message will be revealed.

Instructions for Making Finger Puppets

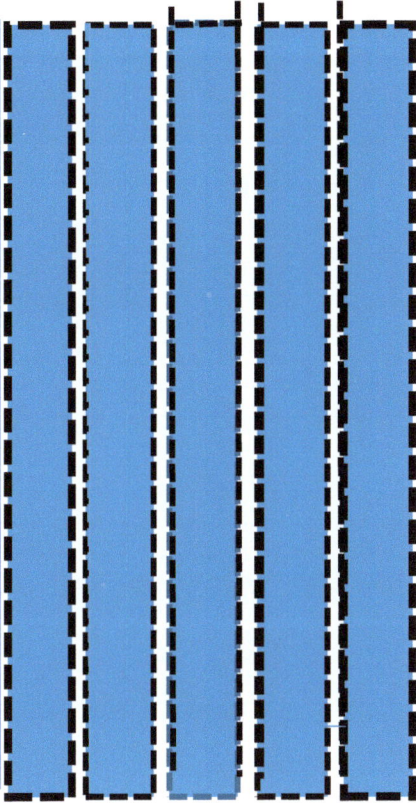

1. Cut figures out.
   Follow the dotted lines.
   lines.

2. Cut strips out. Follow the dotted lines.

3. Fold over strip and tape into a ring.

4. Tape ring on the back of the figure that you cut out.

Cut Out the Finger Puppets

Dove Letter Cutout

Cut Out the Finger Puppets

Receive a *15% discount coupon* off of the purchase of my Editor's Edition of "**The Spirit of Truth**" Storybook Series, with proof of purchase from A - Z. This special edition will contain all 26 stories within two volumes, along with some added goodies. Fill out the chart below, and **please print** all information clearly.

A	B	C	D	E	F
G	H	I	J	K	L
M	N	O	P	Q	R
S	T	U	V	W	X
Y	Z				

Glue your "**Dove Letter**" cutouts in the corresponding boxes, on top of the proper letter. Fill 26 spaces from A- Z. Then cut this page out and mail it to:

Linda Mason
P. O Box 1162
Powhatan, VA 23139

Name _____

Address_____ State: _____

Zip_____

Email
Address_____

Spirit of Truth Storybook Series

APPROPRIATE AGE LEVEL

COLOR CODING KEY

The reading level for these stories is grade five, but they can be understood and enjoyed by the ages listed below, sometimes needing to be read to by someone older.

Ages 4 and 5 = GREEN

Ages 6 and 7 = BLUE

Ages 8 and 9 = ORANGE

Ages 10 and above = RED

A unique inspirational message has been coded throughout each story to help create 'added focus,' as well as a visual tool for interactive concentration. **Decode your secret message (written in red lettering throughout the story)** *and send* *it to me, along with your name and age, through my email address on my website, www.BooksByLMason.com, and you will receive a personal email response from me. Some of the letters of the secret message have already been provided to assist you in your decoding. Additionally, added bonuses of finger puppet activities, brain games, puzzles, or other goodies, awaits each reader in the back of every storybook. A delightful "Treasure Hunt" can be found throughout the illustrations from my collection of storybooks, which* **details can only be found on my website.**

Also, E-Book Editions of this collection of storybooks, having no activities in the back of the books, and a Collector's Edition of this 26 Storybook Series is forthcoming. The collector's edition will include all 26 stories in two volumes, at which time, the Master's List of every inspirational message will be revealed.

Synopsis of Each Story from A-Z

1. *Anxious Arlene:* This story is about a set of rambunctious siblings who live with their loving grandparents, and an adorable, adopted mutt experiencing a few mishaps. This story is recommended for ages five and up.

2. *Busy Benny:* Benny is a dynamic little boy who loves to tinker with wacky car models. He enters a neighborhood race one day with an interesting, wacky race car designed by himself, with the help of his parents. It's also a story about friendship. This story is recommended for ages seven and up.

3. *Catty Carla:* This story is told through the eyes of cats and deal with one cat in particular, with a "Catty" attitude. The

insults are released upon another cat that has a severe physical illness. The gossiper soon regrets the spiteful attitude and adjusts her behavior before the very sick cat transitions to "Kitty Heaven." The story does deal with the death of a pet gracefully. This story is recommended for ages five and up.

4. *Doubtful Denise:* A divorced father is raising his bi-racial daughter, who, at the moment, is full of self-doubt and lacks confidence in her ability to complete any assigned task. Through the love of her father and some very positive friends, Denise learns to believe in herself eventually. This story is recommended for ages seven and up.

5. *Excited Ernesto:* This story is about an average teen who has a fear of riding Roller Coasters. With the help of some of his friends, who also have that same fear, they work through it all at the county fair. This story is recommended for ages seven and up.

6. *Fearless Freddie:* A little boy who loves taking a risk, reminds his father of himself

when he was young. Freddie went too far one day and ended up with a severe injury, but will this stop his risky behavior or give him new ideas to participate in more dangerous stunts? This story is recommended for ages five and up.

7. *Graceful Gregory:* This story highlights the life of a young male teen who has been hassled at school because he loves creative dancing instead of football. Even his football-loving dad sometimes doesn't understand Gregory's love of ballet, jazz, and the many other facets of creative dance. One day, Gregory and his dad work things out with the help of ane teen friend who learns to appreciate the physical strength and courage it takes to become a great dancer. This story is recommended for ages seven and up, but younger if the child is already dancing.

8. *Hopeful Henry:* This story is one example of how staying "hopeful" even through rough times, always pays off. This story is recommended for ages seven and up.

9. *Itchy Irvin:* This story plays out through a pack of dog characters who encounters a

little boy with a physical problem that resembles that of his own. The dog and the little boy meets, and beautiful things begin to happen. This story is recommended for ages seven and up.

10. *Jumping Josey:* This story is about a young teen who lives a life of thrills as a cheerleader. Her hobby takes her into the arena of skydiving. This new adventure eventually leads her to a career in the Armed forces. This story is recommended for ages seven and up.

11. *Kissing Kirkland:* A very "Cutesy" story about a little boy who is infatuated with kissing every animal he comes around, including bugs. This story can is recommended for children ages five and up. This story is recommended for ages five and up.

12. *Lonely Lucilia:* This story deals with teen friendships and having to separate due to a parent's job relocation from one country to another: England to the USA. You can survive when your heart has been broken, even as a child. This story is recommended for ages eight and up.

13. *Muddy Maria:* This story tracks the life of two little girls who loved to play in the mud as children. This love of "dirty play" eventually led them to a lucrative child business dealing with plants. This story is recommended for ages five and up.

14. *Noisy Nelly:* This story is told through the eyes of a bird who learns, by the wisdom of its mother, that life is much more than things perceived as "gloomy." When you learn to see things from a different perspective, you can soar. This story is recommended for ages seven and up.

15. *Orphaned Ophelia:* Most of this story takes place in a very unique orphanage where several unrelated girls experience different lonely situations, as they all long to be adopted by a family they can call their own. Travel with Ophelia through ups and down in an exciting but lonely place where sometimes there are happy endings. This story is recommended for children ages five and up.

16. *Pudgy Pete:* This story intertwines the life of a slightly plump teen boy with self-esteem issues and an enthusiastic teen girl

who just moved in next door. She happens to use a wheelchair. Through the interactions of these two individuals, Pete's self-esteem takes on a new course, and he learns to see himself more than a plus pants size. This story is recommended for children ages seven and up.

17. *Quarrelsome Quaniqua:* This story contains **sensitive** material, and is not intended to be read as a *bedtime* story. It deals with an abusive living environment (non-sexual but very much physical abuse). There are some hard times happening; however, Quaniqua does figure out, with the help of some new friends, how to turn her situation around. This story is recommended for children eight and up; however, please use parental wisdom as to if this story is suited for your particular child.

18. *Reckless Ricardo:* This story is about a young boy experiencing a reckless, behavioral unbalance due to a peanut allergy. A doctor didn't detect this. In searching the internet, one day, his grandmother (his caretaker) discovers the

real issue of dealing with Ricardo. Through a creative experiment, she was able to steer Ricardo's behavior in a more positive direction. This story can be enjoyed by children ages seven and up.

19. *Shy Stanley:* This story gives you a glimpse into the life of a tranquil little boy who has a unique talent. He channels his energy into drawing. He eventually meets a young girl who has similar skills, and they soon develop a quiet bond. This story can be enjoyed by children ages seven and up.

20. *Tearful Tanya:* This story deals with a little girl who is full of grief over the passing of her grandmother. The family has a spiritual upbringing, and Tanya's mom guides her through the grieving process as she draws strength from above, where she's convinced her grandmother now resides. This story may be a little sensitive if you are a child in a similar situation, yet it can be enjoyed by children ages five and above.

21. *Ungrateful Ursula:* This story contains '**sensitive**' material and is recommended for children ages ten and above. Ursula has

become accustomed to using "Cutting" to cope with her many issues of life. Walk with her as she moves from "much pain" to "much gain." She eventually discovers a better way of coping with adversity with the help of her once absent father.

22. *Valiant Vivica*: This story is about a very gifted little girl who loves contact sports to the point of joining a coed wrestling team. Her life is interrupted by a tornado during a wrestling tournament at school. This experience changes her overall focus; however, she remains a top athlete in anything she chooses to pursue even though her aspirations have changed. This story can be enjoyed by children ages eight and above.

23. *Worrying Winston*: If you enjoy treasure hunts, you will love this story. Winston lives with his father while his mom serves in the Marine Armed Forces. They have a unique family unit, but one day Winston's worries come to pass when he gets news from the Armed Forces concerning a severe injury involving his mom. This situation changes their entire world. However, they survive.

This story can be enjoyed by children ages eight and above.

24. *X-Con Xavier*: This person is a teen who had to be incarcerated due to destructive behavior caused by a rebellious attitude. Having had an unstable home environment, he had a "So What" attitude. While incarcerated, he encounters an individual that offers him a more positive way of life. What choice will he make? This story is recommended for children ages ten and above.

25. *Yearning Yolanda*: This story gives you a bit of insight through the mind of a young girl who is now blind but wasn't born blind. Walk with Yolanda through an even more formidable challenge as she saves her mother's life during a house fire. Yes, even though she is blind. This story can be enjoyed by children ages eight and above.

26. *Zealous Zeporah*: Zeporah is a very passionate young lady full of enthusiasm for life. She is also a junior coach for her track team at school. She gets injured before a vital track met but never missed a

step in leading her team to the most outstanding scores they have ever achieved. This story can be enjoyed by children ages seven and above.

About The Author

Minister Linda Mason is a unique ministry gift to the Body of Christ. Her experiences include the establishment of *Spirit of Praise Liturgical Outreach, Inc.*, a non-profit 501 © three organization, which not only helped to establish and oversee new dance ministries but also extended into the communities.

In addition to the *Spirit of Truth Storybook Series*, Minister Linda has published *Appetizers from the Word of God, Are You Hungry?* Volumes 1, 2, & 3, which is an excellent tool for teaching foundational truths, simplistically, from God's Word.

Linda is a native of Suffolk, Virginia, the wife of George B. Mason, Jr., the mother of three: Tamara, Tiena, and George III. She has three adorable grandchildren; Niyah, Laana, and Aaron. Linda holds an Associate Degree in Early Childhood Education and has a passion for writing. She has published 26 children's stories from A to Z, in addition to over 50 other books, including five suspense teen novels. Linda plans to have these unique stories available in both English and Spanish soon.

What others have stated about this Series

- *Author Linda Mason's book, "Kissing Kirkland," is one of a series of books that tells a delightful story with a secret hidden valuable message for children. Her stories will captivate her audience with a variety of age-appropriate activities to enhance each child's learning. As an educator for many years, I highly recommend her books!* **By Amelia Hopkins, a high school counselor.**

- *Linda Mason has done an excellent job using her creativity and insight in writing this series of books, the* **Spirit of Truth Storybook Series from A-Z***. Each book deals with a subject or situation, such as a particular disability or setback that a child might encounter and have difficulty dealing with. The books offer resolutions that are positive and encouraging, helping a child build strength, confidence, and maturity. The activities in the back of each book reinforce the lesson learned. The graphics are colorful and eye-catching, and each book's vocabulary is age-appropriate. Each book is color-coded to fit each age group,* *so there are appropriate books for every child's age. These are books your children will want to read or hear over and over, read by a big sister or brother. And they also have the opportunity to communicate with the author directly! I highly recommend these books for your children and grandchildren!*

Nona J. Mason, a retired teacher, mother, and   grandmother.

www.ingramcontent.com/pod-product-compliance
Lightning Source LLC
Chambersburg PA
CBHW042130080426
42735CB00001B/35